J
B
WASHINGT
ON

McKissack, Pat,
1944-

Booker T.
Washington.

$12.95

DATE		

Booker T. Washington

Leader and Educator

Patricia and Fredrick McKissack

Series Consultant: Dr. Russell L. Adams, Chairman,
Department of Afro-American Studies, Howard University

Illustrated by Michael Bryant

❖ *Great African Americans Series* ❖

ENSLOW PUBLISHERS, INC.

Bloy St. & Ramsey Ave. P.O. Box 38
Box 777 Aldershot
Hillside, N.J. 07205 Hants GU12 6BP
U.S.A. U.K.

To Estelle and Mike Smith, Happy Memories

Library of Congress Cataloging-in-Publication Data

McKissack, Pat, 1944-
        Booker T. Washington : leader and educator / Patricia and Fredrick
McKissack.
            p. cm. — (Great African Americans series)
        Includes index.
        Summary: A biography of the former slave who founded Tuskegee
University and later became the most powerful African American
leader at the turn of the century.
        ISBN 0-89490-314-4
        1. Washington, Booker T., 1856-1917—Juvenile literature. 2. Afro-
Americans—Biography—Juvenile literature. 3. Educators—United
States—Biography—Juvenile literature. 4. Tuskegee Institute—
Juvenile literature. [1. Washington, Booker T., 1856-1917.
2. Educators. 3. Afro-Americans—Biography.] I. McKissack,
Fredrick. II. Title. III. Series: McKissack, Pat, 1944- Great
African American series.
E185.97.W4M33   1992
370'.92—dc20
        [B]   92-5356
                                                                                      CIP
                                                                                       AC

Printed in the United States of America

10 9 8 7 6 5 4 3 2 1

Photo Credits: Library of Congress, pp. 4, 16, 27, 28; Fredrick McKissack, pp. 23, 29; National Park Service, U.S. Department of the Interior/Richard Frear, p. 6; U.S. Department of
the Interior, Tuskegee University, pp. 19, 22, 24.

Illustrations Credit: Michael Bryant

Cover Illustration Credit: Ned O.

Contents

Booker T. Washington
Born: 1856, Franklin County, Virginia.
Died: November 14, 1915, Tuskegee, Alabama.

1
From Slavery to Freedom

Booker Taliaferro Washington never knew his birthday. He was born a slave, and the dates of slave births were not always written down. It is believed he was born sometime in 1856.

Booker and his family lived on a large Virginia plantation. Their one-room shack had a dirt floor. The door didn't shut well. The windows had no glass. There were cracks in the walls.

Booker didn't even have a bed. He slept

This is Booker's Virginia birthplace.

on the floor next to his brother John and his sister Amanda. A fireplace warmed the cabin. But it was always too hot or too cold in their home.

When Booker was five years old, his master put him to work. Booker fanned flies away from his master's table at mealtimes.

When he got older, he was given a new job. Every week he went to the mill with

a load of corn. The corn was ground into meal there.

One day Booker passed by a school. He wanted to go inside. But slave children could not go to school. It was against the law!

In 1861 the Civil War began. Northern and Southern states were at war with each other.

Lots of people wanted to end slavery. In

1863, President Abraham Lincoln freed all slaves in the South. But some slaves didn't know they were free until the war ended in 1865.

Northern soldiers came to the plantation where Booker and his family lived. The soldiers said they were free. There was a lot of singing and shouting. Freedom had come at last!

2

From Malden to Hampton

Booker and his family were free. But, life was not much better for them. They could not read or write. They had no money, no jobs, and no home. How would they live? What could they do?

Booker's stepfather took his family to Malden, West Virginia. He found a job at a salt furnace. At the furnace, salt was boiled out of water that came up from under the ground. Booker and his brother shoveled the salt into barrels.

Soon a school opened for black children in Malden. Booker finally got a chance to go to school.

The teacher asked him his name. He gave his first name, "Booker." The teacher wanted to know his last name. Booker did not know what to say. He had never had a last name. He thought a long time about it. Then he told the teacher, "My name is Booker Washington."

Booker had to work, so he didn't go to school often. But he read everything he could.

General Lewis Ruffner owned the salt furnace and coal mines in Malden. He hired Booker to do housework for his wife. Mrs. Ruffner was fussy and hard to please. She wanted everything to be spotless. Booker did his best to please her.

Mrs. Ruffner liked Booker. So, she let

him read her books. She talked to him a lot about going to school.

Booker heard about a school in Hampton, Virginia. He wanted to go there. He worked even harder and saved his money. In the fall of 1872, Booker had enough money. He left Malden to go to Hampton School.

The school was 500 miles away. Booker walked in the rain. He slept on the ground. He hopped trains, and begged for rides on the back of wagons. It was a long, hard trip. But he would not turn back.

3

From Hampton to Tuskegee

Booker finally reached Hampton School. Miss Mary F. Mackie was the head teacher. She told him there were no more openings. But she gave Booker a job. "Sweep the classroom floor. Then I will give you a meal." She left Booker to do the job.

Mrs. Ruffner had taught Booker how to clean a room. He swept the classroom floor three times. Then he dusted it four times.

Miss Mackie came back later. She looked in the classroom and smiled. "There is an opening," she said. Miss Mackie hired Booker to be the janitor. And that is how he worked his way through school.

General Samuel C. Armstrong was the principal of Hampton. Most of the students who came to Hampton had been

slaves. General Armstrong believed that
learning a skill like bricklaying or
carpentry was the best way for African
Americans to better themselves. Booker
believed it, too.

Booker graduated from Hampton
School in 1875. He taught for a while in
Malden and then in another school in
Washington, D.C. Four years later

After Booker graduated from the Hampton School, he helped his brother John and sister Amanda go to school, too. John became a teacher. He and Booker later worked together.

General Armstrong asked Booker to come back to Hampton.

Booker helped teach Native American students. He did the job very well. Booker was put in charge of the adult night school by the end of the next year.

General Armstrong got a letter from a group of people in Tuskegee, Alabama. They needed a principal for their school. General Armstrong gave them Booker T. Washington's name. They offered Booker the job.

4

The Tuskegee Dream

Booker reached Tuskegee in June 1881. He had lots of students. But he did not have a place to hold classes. He did not have any school materials either.

That didn't stop Booker. He held his first class in a Tuskegee church on July 4, 1881. Thirty students came. Booker was the only teacher.

Six weeks passed. The school was still open. Booker hired Miss Olivia Davidson to be his first teacher. She is often called

Olivia Davidson helped raise money to keep Tuskegee open. She later became Booker's second wife. Once, when Booker was away on business, there was a fire in their home. Olivia got all the children to safety, but the strain was too much on her health. She died soon afterward.

the cofounder of Tuskegee. She was in charge of the women students. Everyone called her Miss D.

Three months after the school opened, friends helped Booker buy an old farm. Booker, Miss D., and their students scrubbed and cleaned the old buildings. People gave gifts. Sometimes they gave money. Sometimes they gave food. Booker was happy to get any help he could.

That is how Booker kept Tuskegee School open for a year. His work at Tuskegee became well known. Many people helped to make the Tuskegee dream come true. They gave their time and money.

Booker wanted Tuskegee to be a fine trade school just like Hampton School. And it was. His students were learning

When people came to visit the Tuskegee campus, they were often surprised to find the great Booker T. Washington working in his garden or feeding his chickens.

how to lay brick, cut stone, hang a door, and make a suit. He liked to show visitors around Tuskegee. Most of the buildings were built by Tuskegee students and teachers. They also grew their own food at the Tuskegee farm.

Booker was married three times. His first wife was his childhood friend, Fannie

Carnegie Hall on the campus of Tuskegee University was built in 1901 by students and faculty. It still stands to remind people that Booker T. Washington believed that African Americans were excellent craftsmen.

Smith. They had one daughter, Portia. Later, Fannie had a terrible fall. She died on May 4, 1884.

Booker married Miss D. two years later. They had two sons, Booker, Jr., and Ernest

Davidson. She worked side by side with Booker until she died on May 9, 1889.

Margaret Murray came to Tuskegee to be the new women's principal. She became Washington's third wife in time. They were married on October 12, 1892. He was 36 years old and she was 31.

The Washington family: Booker T., with his third wife Margaret Murray, his daughter Portia, and his two sons, Booker Jr., and Ernest Davidson.

5

From Poverty to Fame

In the 1890s African Americans were losing their right to vote. Unfair laws were being passed that took away many of their civil rights. Frederick Douglass, the most well-known black leader had just died. People were wondering who would be the new black leader.

Booker gave a very important speech at the Atlanta Cotton Exposition on September 18, 1895. He said in his speech that the races could be as separate as the fingers on the hand in all social things. But when the country was in need (such as during war), the races could work together "like the fist."

Afterward Booker T. Washington became the most powerful black leader of that time.

Many white people liked what Booker said. He was the leader they wanted. African Americans were divided. Some agreed with him. Others did not like his ideas. A lot of African Americans did not like white people telling them who their leaders should be.

Booker became a very powerful man. He talked with presidents and rich businessmen. In 1900, he started the National Negro Business League. The group tried to get more black businesses started.

Booker T. Washington told African Americans to build their own houses so they wouldn't be homeless. And he told them to learn how to farm and take care of animals and they would never be hungry.

Booker T. Washington was a very busy man, but he took time to write a book about his life. He called it *Up From Slavery*. He also enjoyed taking care of his garden, fishing, riding his horse, and telling visitors about the Tuskegee dream.

During a trip to New York, Booker

The Tuskegee staff in 1897. It included George Washington Carver, the great peanut scientist (fourth from the left, last row).

became sick. Margaret went to bring him home. Booker T. Washington died a few hours after he got home to Alabama on November 14, 1915.

This well-known statue is on the campus of Tuskegee University. Booker T. Washington is shown "lifting the veil of ignorance from his people."

Words to Know

Atlanta Cotton Exposition—It was a large business and industry fair. The South wanted to show how much progress it had made since the Civil War. It was held in 1895.

businessman—A person who earns money by selling a product or giving a service. Booker T. Washington wanted more black people to start businesses.

civil war—A war fought within a country. The United States Civil War was fought between Northern and Southern states from 1861 to 1865.

Douglass, Frederick—A black leader who worked to end slavery. He died in 1895. Booker T. Washington took his place as the most important black leader in America.

graduate—To finish a course of study at a school.

janitor—A person who keeps a building clean. Booker worked his way through school as a janitor.

National Negro Business League—A group that was started by Booker T. Washington. It was started to help African Americans start more businesses.

plantation—A large farm. When Booker T. Washington was born, plantations were places where slaves worked in the fields.

president—The head of a country or a group.

principal—The head of a school. Booker was the principal of Tuskegee.

salt furnace—A place where salt was boiled out of water brought up from under the ground. The salt was put into large barrels shipped out and sold.

slave—A person who is owned by another person and forced to work for no pay.

trade school—A school where students learn how to be skilled craftsmen, such as carpenters, bricklayers, tailors, and printers.

Index